# Birds in Our Back Garden
## A Nature on Our Doorstep Book

Song Thrush

Annette Meredith (author and photographer)
Barry Stalker (photographer)

# For my grandchildren

Jay

With thanks to Michelle for all her help, to Ben and my brother Ian for their technical assistance
and to Ted for his ever-patient support and advice.
Thanks also to Dominic for the author photo.

Pair of passenger pigeons depicted in mural at International Crane Foundation, Baraboo, Wisconsin.
The mural was created by Victor Bakhtin. (Courtesy Project Passenger Pigeon)
Many thanks to Ian for providing the great tit nest box photos.

## Birds You'll Find in This Book

Green Woodpecker

Wren

Linnet

Pied Wagtail

Starling populations in the UK double in winter, with migrant birds from Europe arriving in autumn. From autumn and through the winter months, huge flocks of starlings often gather at dusk before descending to their favourite roosting sites, perhaps piers or large buildings with ledges, but also reed beds, woods or cliffs.

Flock of Starlings, also known as a "murmuration"

They may just look like dots, but each speck is one starling!

Starlings like to gather and perch on wires. Often, this is something that birds do when they are getting ready to migrate.

## Part One – The Importance of Birds

When we go outside, what do we usually hear? If we're in a park or back garden, one of the sounds is almost always the sound of birds. Even in towns, sparrows and pigeons and other birds peck around on the ground for food or perch on the rooftops and balance on wires. They sing or squawk, chatter or tweet, coo or caw. Imagine a world without the background noise of the birds. It would be very, very quiet.

Part of a flock of Waxwings

Ecosystem – a community of living and non-living things (water, soil, air, plants and everything living) that work together to create a balance. It can be big or small.

Size: 18 – 20 cm

When we see plenty of birds, it tells us that the environment is probably healthy and safe for other creatures too. When there are not many birds, or fewer than there used to be, it may be an important sign telling us to look closely to see if there have been any changes in the local ecosystem. It may be vital to take action and help to look after the wildlife so that birds and other creatures can survive. We can all help to protect birds, even if we only help those in our own gardens.

It's very easy to take birds for granted. We expect them to be there and we haven't always realised what can happen if they disappear. About fifty years ago, we began to notice the effect of pesticides on the environment, especially on birds. Since then, many organisations have been created to spread the message that we must protect the environment and everything in it. Today, that message is more important than ever.

The size of a bird is its length from the tip of its bill to the tip of its tail.

Pesticide – a chemical substance or mixture that is designed to kill pests, but may also poison or kill other creatures.

A food chain starts with plant life and ends with animal life. When an animal dies, it goes back into the soil and feeds the plants, completing the circle of life.

Skylark

Size: 15 – 20 cm

Moorhen

When pesticides are sprayed on plants, any creatures on the plants are poisoned. Those insects, caterpillars, spiders and other bugs are all food for birds and small mammals, which are in turn food for other creatures further up the food chain. Pesticides never stay just in the area where they are sprayed; they are carried into the environment and can be there for years.

Predators like hawks are high up in the food chain. If this sparrowhawk catches a smaller bird that has eaten an insect or a seed poisoned by chemicals, it will be affected. Everything in nature is connected.

Predator – an animal or bird that kills and eats other creatures.

Sparrowhawk

Size: 28 - 40cm

Hawks are birds of prey. Look at this sparrowhawk's sharply pointed beak. You can tell a lot about what a bird eats by looking at its bill. Birds of prey have sharp claws called talons.

Humans are at the top of the food chain. When pesticides are used, they are carried into the air, soil and water and they affect everything in the ecosystem, including people.

150 years ago, there were more passenger pigeons in North America than any other bird. Nobody believed that they could ever be in danger of extinction, because there were millions or even billions of them. They would travel together in flocks so large that they would darken the sky and they made such a loud noise that people outside would often run indoors! Always travelling and roosting in large groups made it very easy for people to catch them and kill them and lots of people hunted them to sell as meat. By 1900 there were only a few left and just over 100 years ago, in 1914, the last known passenger pigeon died at the Cincinnati zoo.

Mural of a Pair of Passenger Pigeons

Today, hundreds more species of birds are in danger. Some, like the passenger pigeon, have already become extinct, but others could still be saved if people take action to protect them.

Birds that can only live in one kind of habitat are especially sensitive to changes in the environment. Thrushes feed on the ground, where they look for snails, worms and insects. Many birds like thrushes are losing their habitat because of human activity, including pollution of the environment by pesticides and herbicides and the clearing of land for construction.

Size: 21 – 23 cm

Song Thrush

Song thrushes eat snails and get them out of the shell by using a small stone as an anvil. Once they've found a good stone, they use the same stone every time.

Song thrushes like to sing from high branches of trees and their songs are some of the most beautiful and varied of any bird. The number of thrushes has fallen to less than half of what it was forty years ago and we should do all we can to help them. One way is to avoid using pesticides.
It is believed that as many as one out of every eight species of birds in the world is in danger of slipping towards extinction, unless we take more care of the environment and make sure that we don't upset the delicate balance of nature.

# Part Two – If You Feed Them, They Will Come

It's very hard to sneak up on a bird. They have really good eyesight and hearing. If a bird sees any sudden movement or hears the slightest unusual sound, it will sound the alarm and every bird in the area will fly away and hide. Birds are always on the lookout and as soon as you open your back door, they will usually disappear. They are still there, you just won't see them. Most can blend in with their surroundings, and the shrubs and trees seem to swallow them up.

Treecreeper

Size: 12.5 cm

Treecreepers are so well camouflaged against tree bark that they can safely roost at night by tucking themselves into a crevice in the bark of a tree trunk.

This tiny wren is hiding in a tussock of grass. Wrens have very loud voices and so they are often heard before they're seen.

Wren

Size: 9 - 10cm

There are three things that all birds need: food, water and shelter, or cover. The more you have that the birds need, the more birds you will bring to your garden.

Camouflage – blending with your surroundings so that you can't easily be seen.

Then, all you have to do is find ways to bring them out into areas where you can see them, without putting them in danger from predators.

An easy way to attract more birds to your garden is to put out food and water. Place feeders near a window and you'll have a better chance of seeing the birds up close, especially if you are patient enough to sit quietly. If you have a large garden, you can hang feeders further away from the house and you'll attract some of the more shy birds. Some birds eat only seeds; they are the vegetarians of the bird world. Others will eat both seeds and insects and some only eat insects or meat.

Top foods for attracting birds to your garden:
* Black oil sunflower seeds
* Nyjer seed (sometimes known as thistle seed)
* White millet
* Cracked corn
* Meal worms (live or dried)
* Peanut butter (best if mixed with cornmeal)
* Suet cakes and birdseed balls

Female House Sparrows

Blue Tit at peanut feeder

Goldfinch

Great Spotted Woodpecker

Many seed eaters feed their chicks insects and bugs, which are high in protein. Most garden birds love sunflower seeds, (black oil sunflower seeds are best); if you hang out a suet cake as well, you'll attract insect eaters too.

7

Birds are easily scared away, because they are always wary and on the lookout for predators. Open spaces mean danger to them and they like to have places to hide, like bushes, shrubs, trees and long grass.

It's important to hang feeders not only where you can see them, but also where it's safe for birds. They need to be able to fly quickly to a nearby bush or tree if they sense danger, so there should be places for them to perch and areas for them to hide. Make sure the feeders are far enough off the ground that cats and other predators can't reach them. Position them close to a window (three feet or less) because when they are placed further away, birds may fly straight into the reflection of the sky in the glass.

This goldcrest flew into a glass window and stunned itself. The photo was taken as it slowly recovered - a few minutes later, it flew away. The goldcrest is Britain's smallest bird – you can see how tiny it is in this photo, compared to a person's hand.

Size: 9 cm

Goldcrest

Birds will also be attracted to your garden if you provide clean water for them. Birds usually visit birdbaths to drink the water. They also need water to bathe in because it is important for them to keep their feathers clean. Birds preen often, to keep their feathers in tip-top condition for flying. In winter, water often freezes and so putting out some warm water for birds to drink may make all the difference to them.

Wood Pigeon enjoying a shower.

Once you start watching the birds and helping them to survive by providing them with food, water and shelter, you'll be rewarded with more and more birds coming to your garden. Soon, you'll learn to tell them apart, you'll find out what they like to eat, and you'll know their names.

To begin with, birds may sometimes all look the same to you, but if you're a good detective you'll soon learn their names and see how different they really are. Start by collecting clues. Take a photo, if you can!

Where did you see the bird? On the ground, in a tree?

What was it doing? Was it eating? If so, what?

What was its main colour? Any other colours?

Did it have any speckles, stripes, or patches of colour?

How big was it? Did it have a long or short tail?

What shape was its beak?

Did it have any unusual features?

Did you hear it sing, or make any sounds?

Was it by itself, or with another bird or birds?

The kingfisher's bill looks like a spear, but kingfishers catch fish with their beaks open. The shape of their beak is what enables them to hit the water at high speed without making a ripple.

Kingfisher

Size: 17 cm

Make a note of the date you spot a particular bird.
You may find that some birds only visit you at certain times of year.

Let's take a look at some of the birds you might see from your window, in your garden, or in the park.

Birds move around a lot, and many migrate. Even when they don't, they may move to different areas in their search for food. If you make them welcome they may choose to live in your garden, but some of the birds will only be around at certain times of year. Some birds will be with you in spring and summer; others will arrive as the summer migrants leave in autumn.

The seasons bring big changes to everyone's garden. Not only do we see different birds at different times of year, but the birds themselves sometimes look very different, depending on the season.

Some birds forage for food on the ground. You'll often see them scratching in the grass or fallen leaves as they look for insects, grubs and seeds. Other birds are more usually seen in trees, on plants, or at feeders. Woodpeckers, nuthatches and treecreepers are often seen on tree trunks, probing for insects under the bark. Birds like swifts and swallows catch insects in the air as they fly.

Forage – to search for food over a wide area.

Robin

Remember to look up in the treetops and down low on the ground, and to listen for birds singing. Their songs are the way they communicate. Sometimes they are for sounding the alarm; often, they are a way of telling other birds to stay away from their territory. And sometimes, they are just chatting with each other!

It's spring, and this robin is proclaiming his territory. Robins have a clear, sweet voice.

## House Sparrow

House sparrows are common on all continents except Antarctica, so wherever you travel in the world, you have a good chance of seeing one. They are also probably one of the best-known birds, because they like living close to people. Sometimes you'll see them hopping around under outdoor tables at restaurants, or pecking at spilled birdseed in a garden centre. Sparrows eat seeds, but they also eat insects and fruit.

female — House Sparrows — Size: 15 - 17 cm — male

Dunnock — Size: 14.5 cm

Male and female house sparrows look quite different. Notice the little black bib on the male and the creamy eye stripe on the female. Dunnocks are sometimes mistaken for sparrows. You may see them hopping around in your garden, especially if you have a hedge or thick bushes, as they like to search on the ground for insects.

In 1958 the leader of China, Chairman Mao, ordered that sparrows should be killed because they ate the seeds of crops in the fields. What the Chinese didn't realise was that sparrows eat insects and also feed them to their young. When the grain grew, the sparrows were not there to control the insects, which ate and damaged the crops. Many people died in the famine that followed.
The sparrow population gradually recovered, but the Chinese had paid a terrible price. They learned that the balance of nature can be very delicate.

# The Titmice

Blue Tit

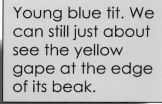

Young blue tit. We can still just about see the yellow gape at the edge of its beak.

Size: 11.5 cm

The small and agile blue tit is one of our best-known and best-loved garden birds. Often the first to find a feeder, the friendly and inquisitive blue tit loves performing acrobatics on the branches of trees as it searches for insects or pecks at buds in spring.  It is about the same size as a coal tit.

Great Tit

Size: 14 cm

The largest of the titmice, the great tit is easily recognised. It has a striking black line down its middle that makes it look like it's wearing a fancy waistcoat. It will come to feeders and may choose your nest box, but it's mainly a woodland bird and you will often spot one if you go for a walk in the woods.

Size: 11.5 cm

Coal Tit

The coal tit looks quite a lot like a great tit, but it's much smaller and not as common. Coal tits are even better at hanging upside down than blue tits, and they are also fond of nest boxes. They eat a lot of insects and in winter they will come for nuts and fat put out in the garden for all the titmice to enjoy.

A tiny bird, the long-tailed tit is well-named because over half its length is made up of its tail. It's mostly black and white with a pinkish breast and is quite often spotted in bushes and shrubs or at suet feeders in gardens.

The long-tailed tit is the only tit that doesn't nest in holes or nest boxes. Instead, it weaves an intricate nest of moss, lichens and cobwebs and lines it with masses of feathers. The nest is attached to twigs and stalks in dense undergrowth and when it's finished it looks like a big, grey-green ball with a round hole near the top. The spider silk is strong and elastic so that the nest can expand as the chicks grow.

In winter, long-tailed tits gather in small flocks and move around looking for food, roosting in thick shrubbery and huddling together at night for warmth.

Long-tailed Tit

Size: 14 cm

# The Finches

Chaffinch

Size: 15 cm

male

The colourful chaffinch is the most common finch in Britain. The female is more of a soft, grey-brown but she still has the black and white bars on her wings. In flight, look for the flash of the white outer tail feathers. Also, listen for the distinctive "pink, pink" call that chaffinches make.

Greenfinches will visit feeders, especially in winter, and like all finches, they love sunflower seeds. The male greenfinch is an olive-green bird with bright yellow markings on its wings and tail; the female is more of a dull brown, but still has the yellow markings. Their beak is the typical finch bill: powerful, chunky, triangular and good for cracking shells to get at the seeds inside.

Greenfinch

Female (male inset)

Size: 14.5 cm

Size: 14 cm

If you have room in your garden for sunflowers or a patch of teasels, you may well get a visit from these beautiful and colourful birds.

Look at this finch's beak. It's chunky, but it has a fine point. The males have a slightly longer bill than the females and they are experts at extracting seeds from teasels and thistles. They also love the seed from smaller, beautiful flowers like tall verbena and coneflowers. Leave those flowers to go to seed and it will be like putting on a feast for the finches in late summer and autumn.

Goldfinches like to flock together when they are not nesting. The reason birds form a group or a flock is because there is safety in numbers. They can feed without all of them having to constantly be on guard and when one sounds the alarm and they take off in a flock, it's much harder for predators to get to them as they swoop and swirl together. Goldfinches have a lovely song and they twitter and sing constantly, a sound you'll soon learn to recognise.

Crows are big birds and easy to recognise by sight or sound. They are large, black birds, often seen in towns and parks. Even before you see them, you can often hear them; their rasping, hoarse "caw" is loud and very distinctive. They will sometimes come to gardens to eat scraps, seeds and suet, but they are ground foragers and too big to eat from feeders. All members of the crow family are intelligent and good at solving problems. Have you ever heard the story of the crow and the pitcher?

Carrion Crow

Size: 48 - 52 cm

Magpie

Size: about 50 cm

Magpies are often seen in parks and gardens and their numbers have increased in recent years. They have a reputation for being thieves – they are probably trying to impress a mate when they pick up shiny objects. They are often considered a nuisance because they are noisy and may drive smaller birds away. They will also rob nests of eggs or chicks.

In Aesop's fable "The Crow and The Pitcher", the crow cleverly works out how to drink from a jug of water. He can't reach the water with his big beak, but by dropping pebbles into the pitcher, the water level rises high enough for him to be able to drink.

Size: 34 - 39 cm

Jackdaw

Jackdaws look similar to crows and rooks, but they are smaller and have a distinctive grey patch on the backs of their heads. When they peer out from a dark nesting place, their startling, pale eyes may be a way of scaring other birds away.

Like crows and magpies, they will eat almost anything, including scraps from rubbish bins. They will also raid nests for eggs or chicks if they can find them; one reason why nests are usually so well hidden.  And they, too, are fond of bright, shiny objects.

Jackdaws live in large groups and will flock together at night to roost. They also like to nest close to each other and here you can see them on a church tower, the sort of place that they consider to be a perfect site for nesting. They have been known to build nests in the chimneys of old houses, even over fireplaces that still work! The only way to stop them is to put a bird guard on the chimney pot.

## Starling

Starlings like to travel around together most of the year and are often seen in a noisy flock perched high in trees, on buildings or wires, or on the ground looking for food.

Iridescent – shining with many different colours from different angles.

Size: 21.5 cm

Starlings will eat almost anything and they can be a nuisance at feeders; some people consider them a pest. In the warmer months they eat mainly insects, worms and caterpillars. They are quite easy to identify, with their iridescent summer plumage and speckled winter feathers.

Starlings often gather in large, noisy flocks. At times, hundreds or even thousands of them congregate and swoop and swirl in the air together. When they fly in tight formation like this, seeming to move as one, it's called a murmuration of starlings and it's an unforgettable sight.

There are so many fewer starlings now than there were thirty years ago that many people are concerned about their future. They may not be as pretty as some of the other birds that come to our gardens, but they are just as important to the ecosystem.

Many species of birds have very descriptive collective nouns for groups of them. Some of the best known are a murder of crows, a charm of finches, a gaggle of geese, a parliament of owls, a host of sparrows and an exultation of skylarks.

# Blackbird

male

female

Blackbird

Size: 25 cm

Male blackbirds are easy to recognise, with their black plumage and bright yellow bill. The female is brown rather than black, but once you know that, it's easy to spot her too. A very common visitor to gardens, a blackbird can become quite tame if you take the time to throw out a few currants or dried mealworms every morning and stay quietly by the door until the blackbird comes to enjoy his breakfast. You may even be lucky enough to have both the male and female come to visit in spring and perhaps build a nest in a low bush or tree in your garden.

This blackbird comes to the back door in winter expecting to be given some food. Snow is on the ground and it's hard for birds to find food when the ground is frozen. He tilts his head and looks expectantly - "Where are my currants?" he seems to be saying.
Blackbirds are often the first to sound the alarm. As soon as other birds hear it, they all fly away.

Wood Pigeon

Feral (town) Pigeon

Size: 31 - 34 cm

Unlike other pigeons, wood pigeons have bands on their neck with a white patch below.

Size: 38 - 43 cm

Pigeons are highly intelligent birds and people have bred them over the centuries for various purposes, including for their meat and as carriers of messages. Even today, pigeons can still be useful for communication in remote areas of the world. Wood pigeons are the largest and most common pigeon in the UK and the one you're likely to see in your garden. The feral pigeon, sometimes called a town or street pigeon, is usually seen in towns and cities. Today's feral pigeons are descendants of rock doves, and they nest on ledges of buildings in towns instead of on cliffs or in caves.

All pigeons like to gather in flocks and their soft, distinctive cooing sound is one that everyone soon learns to recognise.

The collared dove has become a very familiar sight in gardens across Britain, although it is not a native species. It was introduced into the UK in the 1950s from Europe and can now be found just about everywhere.

Collared Dove

Size: 32 cm

Collared doves usually build their nests close to people, in gardens or parks where food is plentiful.

They lay two white eggs. The chicks hatch in about two weeks and fledge about three weeks later. Baby pigeons and doves are called squabs.

You can see what a nest and squabs look like on page 26.

Other pigeons in Britain are the rock dove, found on the coasts of Scotland and Ireland, the stock dove and the turtle dove, which is only in Britain during the summer months. The stock dove looks very much like a feral pigeon, and is often mistaken for one. It is about the same size, but it has a dark back rather than the white back of a feral pigeon, although it's hard to see the colour of its back unless the pigeon is in flight. Next time you spot a pigeon, look at it very carefully and see if you can identify which one it is.

Juvenile Robin

Robin

Size: 14 cm

Everybody loves robins! Nearly everyone knows what a robin looks like, even if it's only because they have seen them on Christmas cards. The male and female look the same as each other, but it would be hard to identify a young robin unless you know what it looks like.

Robins love to sing. They may seem friendly to us, but they are actually singing to proclaim their territory and they are quick to chase off intruders.

Next time you're out in the garden, see if you can spot a robin hopping around in the hedges and under bushes. You can often entice them out with dried mealworms, or if they see you digging, they'll be waiting to come and search for tasty, wormy snacks as soon as you've gone!

## Some Newcomers and Success Stories

Ring-necked Parakeet

Size: 36 – 43 cm

Since the 1990s, ring-necked parakeets have become a common sight and familiar sound in and around London and its suburbs.

They look more like they belong in a tropical rainforest than in England, but parakeets are now widespread in areas around London and their populations are growing. No-one knows exactly how they came to be here; one legend says they escaped from a film set, another that a pop star released a pair, yet another that some escaped after the 1987 hurricane.

The most likely explanation is that they were accidentally introduced into the wild by people who kept them as exotic pets, but whatever the case, they are now thriving. Some people are worried that native birds are losing their habitat as the parakeets take over nesting holes in trees that might have been used by species like woodpeckers and owls, but the parakeets live mainly in urban settings and do not seem to be expanding their range. They like fruit, berries, nuts and seeds, so they will come to feeders and their noise and size can sometimes frighten other birds away. They will peck at buds, blossom and fruit on trees, too.

There is always a risk when a species is introduced to an area where it has never lived before that it may upset the balance in the local ecosystem. The non-native parakeets are beautiful birds, but we don't want some of Britain's native birds to lose their habitat. Conservationists are people who speak out and act to try to make sure that the environment is protected.

Red Kite

Size: 60 - 70 cm

Over 100 years ago, the red kite was in real danger of dying out in Great Britain.

Throughout most of the last century, the number of red kites in Britain remained dangerously low and it wasn't until the 1980s that organisations like the RSPB (Royal Society for the Protection of Birds) took action to bring red kites back to areas of Britain where they had once been common. It has taken several decades, but red kites are now often seen soaring in the skies above us, especially in the Chilterns.

Every year, the RSPB collects information from as many people as possible about bird visitors to gardens and schools. It's fun to take part, and the results tell us a lot about which birds are doing well and which species are increasing or declining. In 2014, for the first time ever, the great spotted woodpecker made it into the top twenty birds most commonly seen in gardens across Britain. Individual species of birds can have a good year, but the top five most common visitors to gardens remain consistent: sparrows, starlings, blue tits, blackbirds and wood pigeons. Even though some bird numbers are declining, we can do a lot to help *all* birds by providing habitat, food and water.

Size: 23-26 cm

Great Spotted Woodpecker

# Part Four – Birds and the Seasons

When it's cold outside, we can wrap up snugly or stay indoors, but birds have to find ways to stay warm through the winter months if they are to survive. Some have to migrate to escape the cold, but a lot of birds are well adapted to deal with the challenges that winter brings, as long as they can find clean water and enough food to give them energy and warmth.

In many parts of the country, January and February mean long, cold nights with temperatures often below freezing. It's at this time of year that taking care of garden birds by providing food and water for them can save their lives. If you provide shelter as well, they will probably stay. You may even be rewarded with seeing them raise their families when spring arrives.

Blackbird

Parakeet

Size: 56 - 66 cm
Herring Gull

Swan

Size: 140 – 160 cm

Frozen ponds can be a challenge!

Birds have several ways to stay warm in winter. Many birds grow extra feathers when they moult in autumn and their outer feathers are waterproof. Birds have downy, insulating feathers growing close to their bodies that keep them warm. Birds' legs and feet are covered with special scales to reduce heat loss and birds shiver to generate body heat. They also eat more in autumn so they can build up body fat to help keep them warm through the winter.

Spring starts early for birds. Birds that stay year round will have been investigating nest boxes during the winter months and by February many have chosen their nesting site. Migrating birds start to arrive and suddenly our gardens are alive with song and colour again. Spring is a time for finding a mate, nesting and raising families. If you wake early enough in the morning, you may hear the "dawn chorus". The birds that have survived the winter now normally enjoy a time of plenty, with insects emerging, flowers blooming and warmer temperatures signalling that winter is over.

Young Collared Doves on the nest

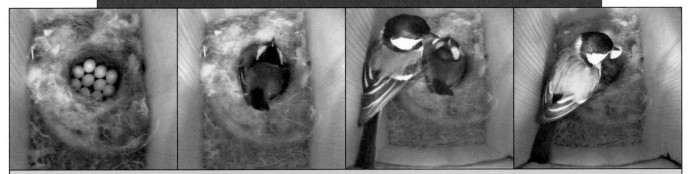

Ten tiny, pale eggs lie in the shelter of the nest box. The female sits on the eggs to keep them warm and the male brings her food. When the chicks hatch, the parent eats the calcium-rich shells. Both parents feed the chicks and keep the nest clean.

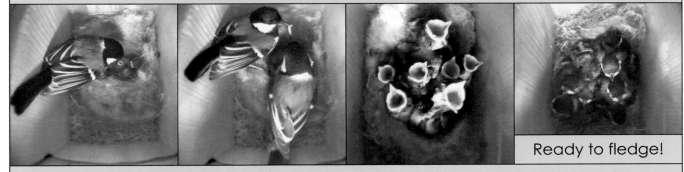

Ready to fledge!

The parents are kept very busy feeding the chicks. Sometimes it takes both of them to divide up the food and they chatter to each other constantly as they attend to their babies, who open their beaks wide as soon as they hear a parent coming.

Here is one of the babies, now a fledgling that has just left the nest. It perches on a branch near the nest box and waits for a parent to bring it something to eat. Now it must practise flying and learn to find its own food. The first few days after a fledgling leaves the safety of the nest are the most dangerous for a young bird.

Birds often have more than one brood in a year. Many fledglings don't survive and those that do still have dangers to face every day.

We should always move quietly near nests and never disturb nesting birds. Fledglings often have mottled feathers to help camouflage them. Young birds rely on their parents to feed them even after they have left the nest, until they learn to find food for themselves.

In spring and summer you may see young birds and wonder what they are, because they often look very different from their parents. The parents may look different from each other, too. Usually, young birds and females are less brightly coloured. If the parent bird gives an alarm call, the chicks know that they must keep very still so that their camouflage makes them hard to see.

Young Blackbird

Birds such as tits and sparrows are cavity nesters and they may nest in boxes we put out for them. Other birds build their nests high up in the trees, or in the dense cover provided by hedges, shrubs or brambles. Some will even nest on the ground; their eggs are always very well camouflaged.

"This looks just right!"

Size: 14 cm

House Martin

Other birds, like house martins, prefer to build their nests right against a wall, under the eaves of a building. Their nests are glued to the wall with mud.

Mallard Ducks

female

male

You've probably seen ducks in parks. Here is the first duck egg in a nest near a pond. Ducks usually have large families, because many young ones don't survive. Ducklings learn to swim before they can fly. Look at how different the adult male and female mallard ducks are.

As the seasons change, birds start to move on. Some stay in the same area, and some families will even stay together through the winter, but most birds move around a lot more than we realise. It's during spring and autumn that we notice the biggest movement of birds as they migrate, and sometimes we may see birds that aren't normally in our gardens.

Look up into the skies in autumn and you may see and hear flocks of migrating ducks or geese flying in a "V" formation.

Many birds travel along coasts and estuaries during migration.

Martins and swallows fly thousands of miles all the way from Africa to spend summer in the UK.

In the UK, about half the species of birds migrate.

Geese

# Part Five – What Would We Do Without Birds?

Throughout history, birds have played an important role in people's lives. During the two World Wars of the last century, homing pigeons were used for carrying messages that brought information which saved many people's lives. Some of the pigeons became quite famous and flew numerous flights into enemy territory.

Birds were the inspiration for us to build machines so that we too can fly, although an airplane cannot match the amazing aerial abilities of a bird. A bird's wings act as both wing and propeller, so it can fly in a much more complicated and varied way than a plane. Different species of birds have different types of wings, from short wings for quick upward movement to long, broad wings for gliding and soaring.

Canaries, parrots, budgerigars and cockatiels are all birds that some people like to keep as pets.

Birds and their eggs have always been an important source of food for people across the world.

Bird feathers have been used for decoration and also for warmth in quilts and clothing. Flight feathers of larger birds can be quills and were used for writing before the invention of pens. Even bird dung, called guano, can be useful; it's been valued as a fertiliser for centuries. Birds have also been an inspiration to artists and scientists since the dawn of civilisation.

Pet Canary

"Canary in a coal mine"- canaries were taken into coal mines so that miners would know that the air was safe to breathe. If the canary stopped singing, they knew that there were poisonous gases that could kill them if they didn't get out straight away. If something or someone is like "a canary in a coal mine", it means that they are giving an early warning of danger to others.

Birds are an essential part of the ecosystem. They pollinate plants, spread seeds and control insect populations by eating bugs. They are part of the food chain as both predators and prey.

Their usefulness to humans as ecological indicators is vital, which means that we need them because watching and studying them tells us a lot about our environment and makes us take notice of problems.

Increasingly, birds are an important source of ecotourism. We don't have to travel to faraway places to enjoy birds, though, because we all have birds in our own gardens and can easily attract more of them.
Look out of your window today and see if you can identify a bird!

Size: 75 - 90 cm

16 cm

Size: 14 cm

Yellowhammer

12.5 -14 cm

Pheasant

Tree Sparrow

Nuthatch

Ecotourism – "Environmentally responsible travel to natural areas, in order to enjoy and appreciate nature" (International Union for Conservation of Nature, or IUCN).

Many birds are best seen early in the morning, but barn owls are most often spotted at dusk.

Barn Owl

Size: 33 - 39 cm

Hawfinches are shy birds that spend most of their time in the treetops. They can crack even the toughest seeds with their massive bill and hornbeams are their favorite tree.

Barn owls can often be seen hovering over rough grassland or along the edges of fields, hunting for voles and other small rodents. Their numbers had declined in the twentieth century due to habitat loss, barn conversions and pesticide use, but populations have been recovering in the last few decades thanks to the efforts of conservationists working with volunteers to put up nest boxes.

Hawfinch

Size: 18 cm

Now you've learned to identify the most common garden birds, you can start looking out for ones that are much harder to find. The hawfinch is probably one of the rarest birds in the UK. If you spot one, you can call yourself an expert birder!

32

# Nature Notes

Sparrow

Collared Dove

Blue Tit

Blackbird

Woodpigeon

Great Tit

Robin

Song Thrush

Goldfinch

Starling

Magpie

Chaffinch

Dunnock

Other birds I have identified:

Greenfinch

Check the boxes when you've identified the birds - you can also add the date and location.
Once you can identify these common birds, you have truly become a birdwatcher!

Start by putting out food and water for the birds. With patience, some of the birds may learn to trust you so that they don't all fly away as soon as you open the door. Always respect your birds' privacy, though, and try not to frighten or disturb them when they are feeding, drinking or bathing.
If you see a young bird on the ground, don't approach it; a parent is almost certainly close by, looking after it.

A pair of binoculars will help you to see a bird in much greater detail so that you'll be able to identify it more easily. Taking photos can also help to show more of the details that make birds look different from each other.
Soon, you'll discover that birds have different personalities, too!

There are many organisations for birdwatchers that are fun to join and lots of information is available in books and online if you want to learn more about a particular bird. Becoming a birdwatcher has never been easier!

Sunflower

Coneflower

Larkspur

Tall Verbena

Zinnia

Cosmos

If you have the space, ask if you can plant some sunflowers in your back garden and later in the year you will have fun watching lots of seed-eating birds cling to the seed heads as they enjoy the feast you have grown for them. Here are some of the flowers that are easy to grow that will attract birds, bees and butterflies.

Make a list of the birds you have seen. If you draw pictures, they will help you to remember a bird's colour and markings. Make a note of where and when the bird was sighted. Keep a nature diary and you will know when you're likely to see all the different birds next year, too.

Greenfinch

Holly Berries

If you're lucky and have a holly tree or hedge, the berries will attract many birds. Feeders are the best way to provide food like sunflower and nyjger seed. In winter, birds need a lot more energy and foods like suet and peanuts provide the calories they need. Even in spring and summer, it's useful for parent birds to have an easy and reliable source of food.
Clean the feeders regularly so that you don't risk making the birds sick.

Young Sparrow

Water attracts many more birds. There are birdbaths you can buy, but it's also easy to make your own from a dish or old flowerpot saucer. Some feeders include a water dish.

Great Tit drinking

In early spring, put out nesting material like twigs, hair, fur, cotton batting, straw and short pieces of string. Mix clay soil and water in an old dish and leave it out, as some birds like to use mud when building their nests.

Be creative!

Put up a nest box in a sheltered place, out of direct sunlight (east-facing is good) and safe from predators. Place it where you can see it from a window. Happy birding!

Leave nest boxes up year round and clean them out after the chicks fledge.

# ABOUT THE AUTHOR

Annette Meredith is a master gardener, photographer and lifelong student of nature who is passionate about environmental issues and conservation. She was born in a small village in England but now lives in North Carolina, where she enjoys encouraging, observing and photographing nature as she works to improve sixty acres of woodland, meadows and organic gardens.

# ABOUT THE PHOTOGRAPHER

Barry Stalker's love of birds has spanned the decades since he was at junior school. He lives in Hampshire, where many of the images in this book were obtained.

*Other Books by Annette Meredith:*

Nature on Our Doorstep (UK)          Nature on our Doorstep (US)
Growing Green Fingers (UK)            Growing A Green Thumb (US)
Saving the Bees                       Birds in our Back Yard (US)
Helping the Hummingbirds              The Secret World of Flowers
Butterflies are Beautiful             A Bluebird Story
The Secret World of Trees             A Nature Companion
The Treasure Hunt (UK)

*For younger readers:*

Nature Rhymes                         Five First Rhyming Readers
Hello, Mr Tibbs

Language learning book: French in Pictures

*www.natureonourdoorstep.com*

Printed in Great Britain
by Amazon